ALTERNATOR BOOKS™

PICTURES to PARAGRAPHS

WRITING AN OPINION PIECE

Heather E. Schwartz

Lerner Publications ◆ Minneapolis

Lerner Publications Company
An imprint of Lerner Publishing Group, Inc.
241 First Avenue North
Minneapolis, MN 55401 USA

For reading levels and more information, look up this title at www.lernerbooks.com.

Main body text set in Aptifer Sans LT Pro.
Typeface provided by Linotype AG.

Editor: Angel Kidd **Designer:** Emily Harris **Photo Editor:** Giliane Mansfeldt
Lerner team: Martha Kranes

Library of Congress Cataloging-in-Publication Data

Names: Schwartz, Heather E. author
Title: Writing an opinion piece / Heather E. Schwartz.
Description: Minneapolis : Lerner Publications, 2026. | Series: Pictures to paragraphs (Alternator Books) | Includes bibliographical references and index. | Audience: Ages 8–12 | Audience: Grades 4–6 | Summary: “Everyone has opinions. It’s important to be able to express those opinions thoughtfully and clearly. By using photos to get readers thinking about their opinions, this guide shows how to write an effective opinion piece”—Provided by publisher.
Identifiers: LCCN 2025013458 (print) | LCCN 2025013459 (ebook) | ISBN 9798765688786 library binding | ISBN 9798348028770 paperback | ISBN 9798765695869 epub
Subjects: LCSH: Persuasion (Rhetoric)—Juvenile literature | Authorship—Juvenile literature
Classification: LCC P301.5.P47 S37 2026 (print) | LCC P301.5.P47 (ebook) | DDC 808—dc23/eng/20250614

LC record available at https://lccn.loc.gov/2025013458
LC ebook record available at https://lccn.loc.gov/2025013459

Manufactured in the United States of America
1-1012673-54708-6/24/2025

TABLE OF CONTENTS

THE POWER OF OPINION

Katie didn't like doing her homework. She wrote an opinion piece explaining why and brought it to the school newspaper. It felt satisfying to put her thoughts in writing.

Writing an opinion piece is a powerful way to express yourself and influence others. First, writers identify their opinions and make a plan for how they want to express their thoughts to readers. Next, they draft a piece that includes both opinions and facts. Facts can be proved with objective evidence that is not influenced by personal beliefs.

Writers then share their draft with readers, such as friends and classmates, to get feedback. This helps writers evaluate their piece and decide how to revise it. Lastly, writers edit their work to fix mistakes. After that, a writer might publish their piece.

An opinion piece has power. It can convince others to act. It may even change the world.

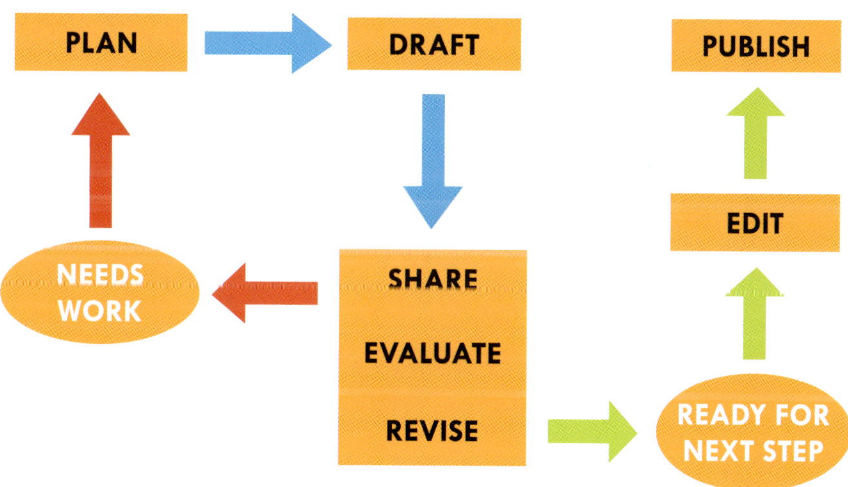

CHAPTER 1
GETTING STARTED

Planning your opinion piece starts with a subject or situation you care about. Consider your daily life at home or at school. Is there anything that makes you feel excited, angry, frustrated, happy, or confused? Current events and causes you believe in can also spark strong emotions.

When this happens, it's a sign you have a strong opinion to express. This could be a good subject for your opinion piece.

Once you have a subject to write about, an outline can help you organize your thoughts and ideas so you can communicate them clearly to readers. The outline is a plan for your draft. It needs an introduction, ideas for body paragraphs, and a conclusion.

Try talking to friends to hear their opinions about your subject.

When you introduce your topic, you want to clearly state what subject or situation you will be covering in your piece. But your introduction doesn't need to be dull. In fact, it shouldn't be! A powerful opinion piece comes from the heart. It's about expressing strong feelings, and that starts with drawing readers in.

One way to introduce your topic is by telling readers about a personal experience you've had. Personal experiences provide subjective evidence for your opinion. They also give you a chance to connect with your topic and write about it with genuine feeling.

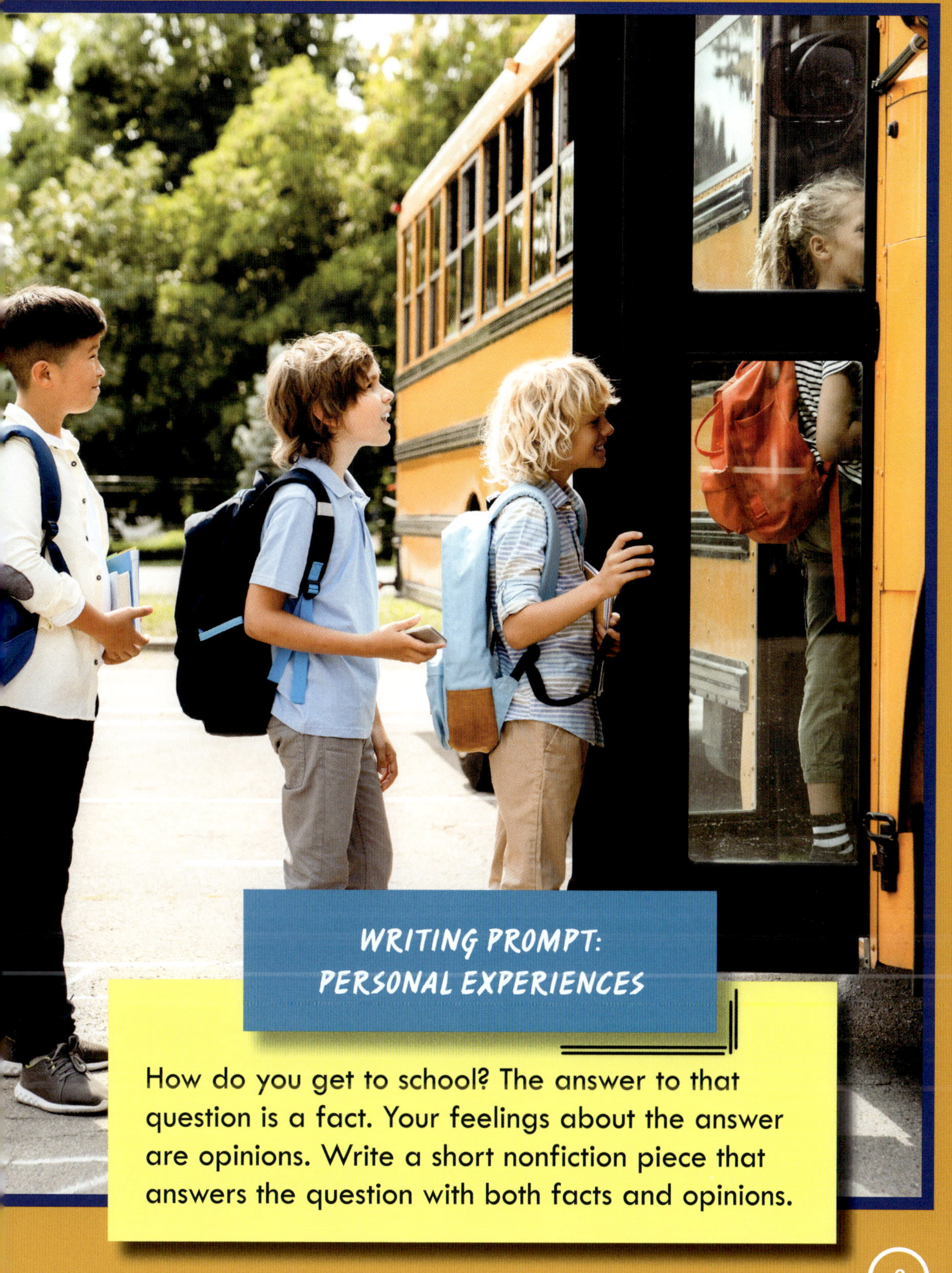

WRITING PROMPT: PERSONAL EXPERIENCES

How do you get to school? The answer to that question is a fact. Your feelings about the answer are opinions. Write a short nonfiction piece that answers the question with both facts and opinions.

When outlining your draft, it helps to also think about your readers' experiences. They might have had experiences that are the same as yours. But that doesn't mean you can assume they feel the same way about them. You may still have to work hard to try to convince readers that your opinion has value—and maybe even change their minds.

Consider what evidence your readers might need. Do they need more facts about the subject? Or do they need more information about why you feel the way you do? This evidence belongs in your body paragraphs. Plan for three to five body paragraphs that include both objective and subjective evidence.

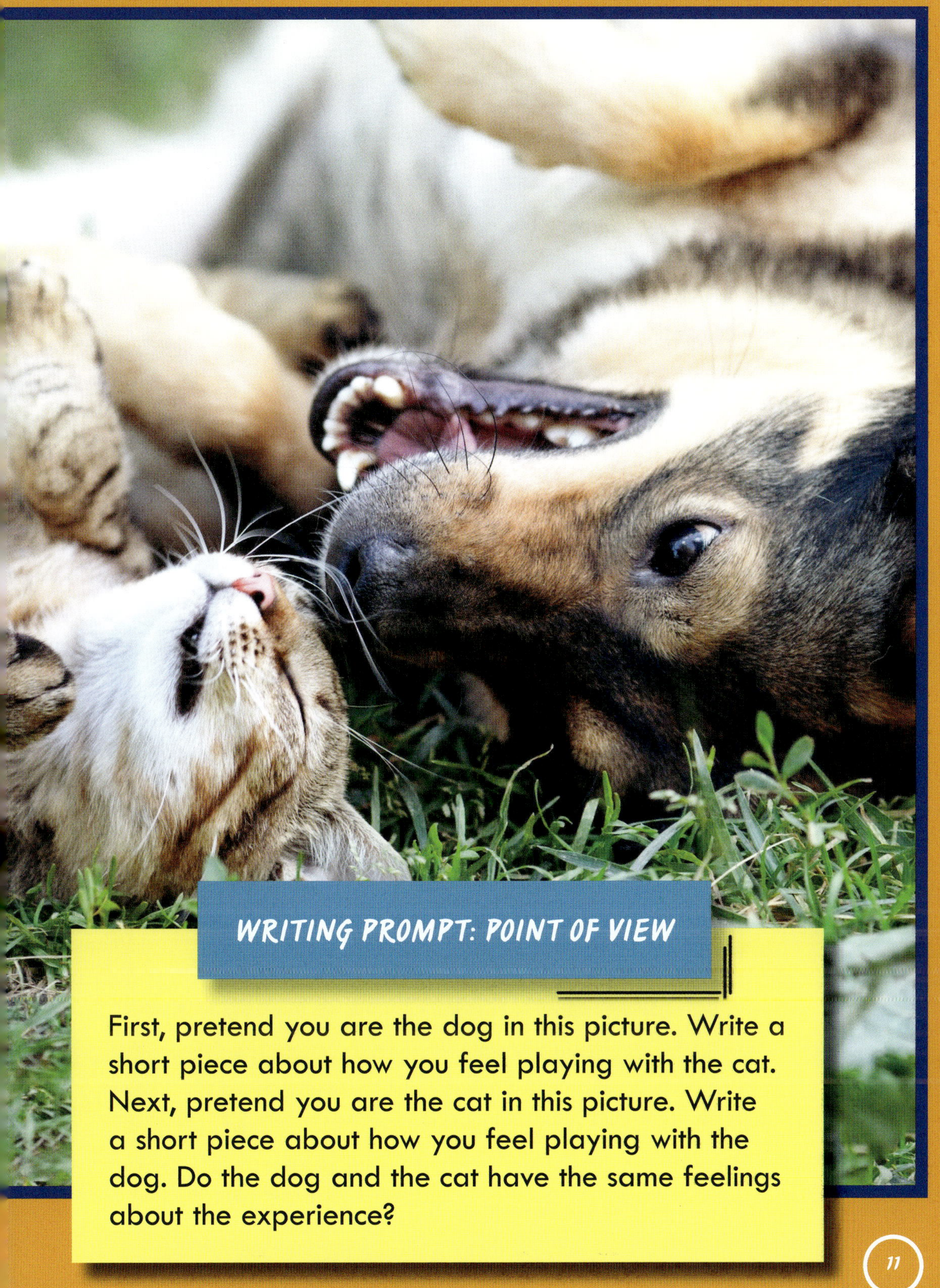

WRITING PROMPT: POINT OF VIEW

First, pretend you are the dog in this picture. Write a short piece about how you feel playing with the cat. Next, pretend you are the cat in this picture. Write a short piece about how you feel playing with the dog. Do the dog and the cat have the same feelings about the experience?

If you have strong feelings about a subject, you're probably not alone. Readers might also have strong feelings about the same subject. They may agree or disagree. No one's feelings are right or wrong. But your body paragraphs can still make a strong case for your own opinion.

WRITING PROMPT: OTHER OPINIONS

Art often evokes different emotions for different people. Write a short piece about what different people might be thinking and feeling about the artwork in this photo.

From introduction to conclusion, it's important to respect your readers even if you suspect they may disagree with you. Rather than trying to prove them wrong, focus on presenting your objective and subjective evidence. Use your piece to express how you feel and why.

WRITING PROMPT: RESPECT FOR READERS

Pretend you and a friend played a game together and you lost. Then your friend gloated about their victory! Write a short message to your friend about how their behavior made you feel.

CHAPTER 2
GATHERING INFORMATION

Before you write your draft, you'll need to research facts and details about your topic. That way, you can present an informed opinion about it. This knowledge will also help you communicate clearly with readers, who may not know as much about the subject as you do.

Consider questions you have about your topic. Then look for answers. The library is a great place to start. You could also speak with an expert. You may be able to gather some information from personal experience. But even if you think you know the facts about a subject, it's important to check them to be sure your information is correct.

Keeping a list of facts and where you found them can be helpful when researching.

Look for facts that support your opinion as well as facts that don't. That way, you'll understand your topic better. Even if you believe the information you found supports your point, check the information you find with reliable sources. Some sources, such as artificial intelligence, may be less trustworthy than others, such as historical documents. If an expert didn't write the piece or check the source, avoid using the information.

WRITING PROMPT: FIND THE FACTS

Write a list of facts and details about a beach that you have visited or would like to visit. What kinds of clothing do people wear? What does the weather feel like? Is the weather the same every day?

Writing your first draft allows you to express yourself and flesh out the points you identified in your outline. You should make your introduction at least one full paragraph. Then write three to five body paragraphs to explore and present your ideas. Your conclusion should also be a full paragraph.

When you're gathering facts and details, you might wind up with so much information you can't possibly fit it all into your piece. Not everything you learn while researching will belong in your piece, even if it is interesting. Too much extra information could detract from your main points and your overall message.

It's important that your opinion piece picks a side and sticks to it. It's not your job to present a balanced argument for opposing opinions. That would be extra information too.

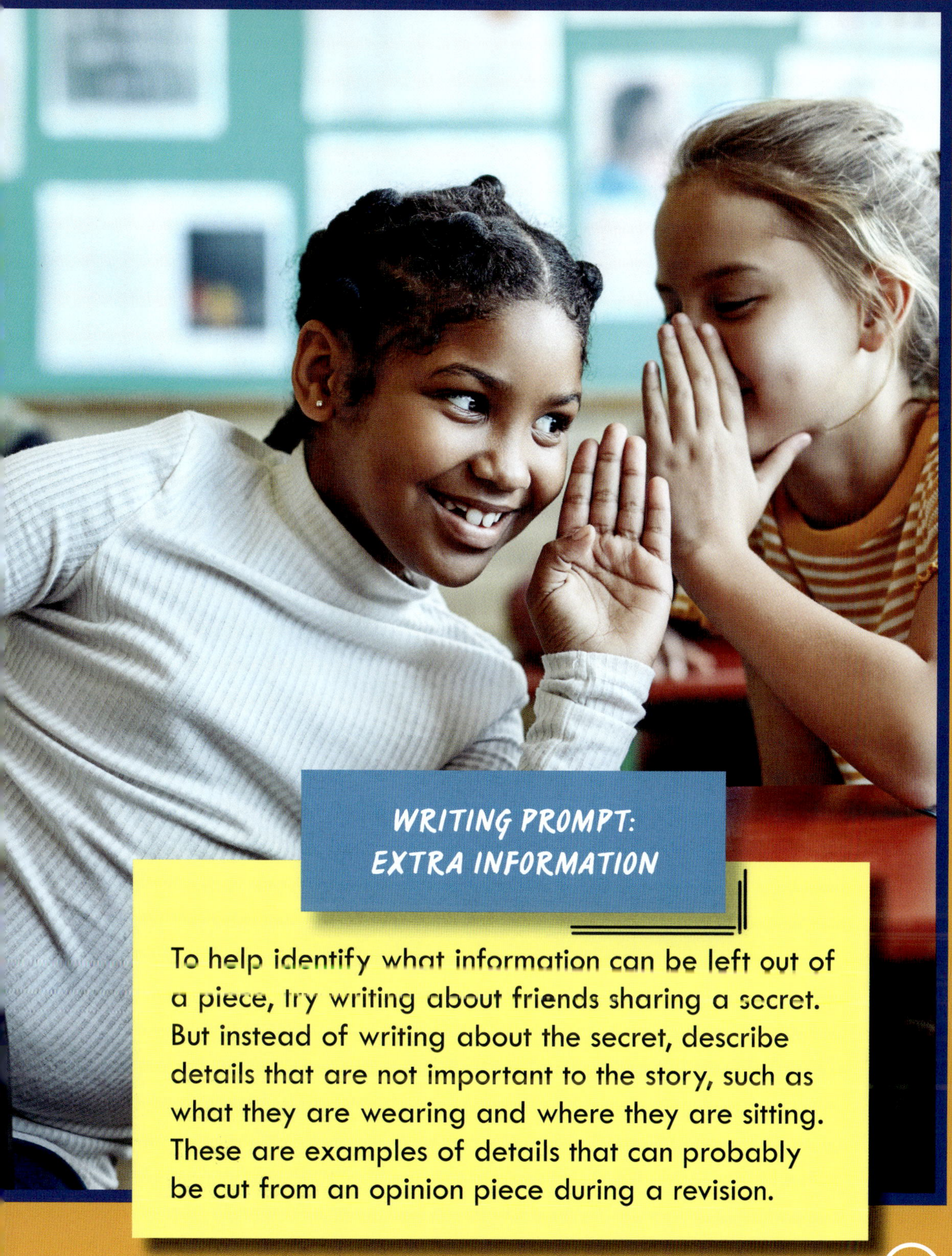

WRITING PROMPT: EXTRA INFORMATION

To help identify what information can be left out of a piece, try writing about friends sharing a secret. But instead of writing about the secret, describe details that are not important to the story, such as what they are wearing and where they are sitting. These are examples of details that can probably be cut from an opinion piece during a revision.

Deciding which facts and details to include is a process. For your first draft, consider whether the information you have will help readers understand your subject. Also think about the opinions you want to express. When a fact or detail directly relates to your opinions, it belongs in your piece.

Sometimes opposing opinions belong too, particularly if they are more popular than your own. But if you do include any opposing opinions, don't argue in favor of them. Use them to prove why your opinion is better. Just make sure to back up your opinion with objective and subjective evidence. While you're writing, you may discover you don't have enough information and need to do additional research.

WRITING PROMPT: NECESSARY KNOWLEDGE

Imagine you are writing a journal entry about a submarine voyage where you saw many types of tropical fish. Describe a few different fish, including important details about how they look.

CHAPTER 3

MAKING A STRONG CASE

After you finish your opinion piece, you can share it with readers to get their feedback. They can tell you what they liked and disliked. They might have questions. If so, you may need to explain some ideas more clearly or rearrange them.

Readers might also critique your writing style. If your sentences all sound similar, you may decide to mix up your sentence structures. You could link ideas with transition phrases. You could also add questions and humor to your piece.

It can be hard to hear negative feedback when you're working on a piece of writing. But try to listen and take it all in. This feedback will help you become a better writer!

WRITING PROMPT: ACCEPTING FEEDBACK

Pretend you are a bird watching a human fill a bird feeder for you. Write a short piece about how accepting help from humans makes you feel. Would you appreciate it? Or would you wish that you were able to find all your own food? Think about how these feelings are similar to emotions that come up when receiving feedback on your writing.

Reader feedback is valuable. But you do not have to incorporate every idea or note into your piece. After all, readers may have many different ideas. And you may not agree with all of them. Be sure to only include feedback that helps the piece express what you want to say. You may decide on your own to cut facts, add details, or change your writing style.

Feedback from a teacher is a little different from reader feedback. A teacher often acts as an editor, offering corrections and suggestions that will make your piece better. When you edit, it usually makes sense to incorporate these ideas. But if you disagree with them, have a talk with your teacher to explain why and learn more.

WRITING PROMPT: EDITING FOR CLARITY

Write the steps for a simple activity, such as brushing your teeth. Read it over and ask yourself if a small child could follow these directions. Consider whether you need to add or cut information or reorder the steps to make them clearer.

After revising and editing, you might get the chance to publish your piece. That means more readers will learn your opinion and maybe even agree with it. You can use your conclusion to wrap up your ideas. Restate your overall opinion as well as some of the evidence you presented in your body paragraphs.

At the very end, consider how you can keep readers engaged even after they've read your piece. For example, you could ask a question that keeps readers thinking about your topic. Or you could offer a call to action they might be willing to accept.

These photos and prompts are just a few ideas to inspire an opinion piece. Throughout your life, you may have strong feelings, beliefs, and judgments about many things. When you want to express yourself on a topic—and connect with others—just put the writing process to work!

WRITING PROMPT: CALL TO ACTION

Imagine you want your opinion piece to inspire real-world action. Write a friendly email to friends about why it's important to clean up litter in a local park. Include both your opinion and some facts.

GLOSSARY

artificial intelligence: a computer system or software that imitates intelligent human behavior

call to action: a next step that the reader could take after reading

critique: to determine what is good or bad about a piece

draft: an early version of a piece of writing

edit: to correct or improve a piece of writing

evaluate: to carefully review, study, or judge something, such as a piece of writing

feedback: opinions, corrections, or comments given to a writer by a reader

objective evidence: evidence that is based on real facts

opinion: thoughts, feelings, and judgments about an issue or subject

publish: to make a piece of writing available to the public

revise: to change or rewrite something to improve it

subjective evidence: evidence that is based on or influenced by personal beliefs

LEARN MORE

Carser, A. R. *What Is Fake News?* BrightPoint, 2023.

Eason, Sarah, and Louise Spilsbury. *How Do I Write Well?* Cheriton Children's Books, 2022.

Fact Protocol: Objective Facts vs. Subjective Facts or Claims
https://fact.technology/learn/difference-objective-facts-vs-subjective-facts/

Schwartz, Heather E. *Writing a Report*. Lerner Publications, 2026.

Time for Kids: Opinion
https://www.timeforkids.com/g56/sections/opinion/

Worksheet Zone: English Language Arts
https://worksheetzone.org/blog/category/english-language-arts

INDEX

PHOTO ACKNOWLEDGMENTS

Image credits: Justin Paget/Getty Images, p. 4; PeopleImages.com - Yuri A/Shutterstock, p. 6; FangXiaNuo/Getty Images, p. 7; Inside Creative House/Getty Images, pp. 8–9; vvvita/Shutterstock, pp. 10–11; Pascal Deloche/Getty Images, pp. 12–13; ibnjaafar/Getty Images, pp. 14–15; DaniloAndjus/Getty Images, p. 16; damircudic/Getty Images, p. 17; Twenty47studio/Getty Images, pp. 18–19; LumiNola/Getty Images, pp. 20–21; SHansche/Getty Images, pp. 22–23; SolStock/Getty Images, p. 24; alexei_tm/Shutterstock, p. 25; Goodboy Picture Company/Getty Images, pp. 26–27; Maskot/Getty Images, pp. 28–29. Design elements: Olex Runda/Shutterstock; Claudio Divizia/Shutterstock.

Cover: LumiNola/E+/Getty Images.

curio?idad por

EL DERRIBE DE NOVILLOS

POR RACHEL GRACK

AMICUS LEARNING

¿Qué te causa